SCIENCE BUZZWORDS

Does It Bounce?

D1318401

For a free color catalog describing Gareth Stevens Publishing's list of high-quality books and multimedia programs, call 1-800-542-2595 (USA) or 1-800-461-9120 (Canada). Gareth Stevens Publishing's Fax: (414) 225-0377. See our catalog, too, on the World Wide Web: http://gsinc.com

Library of Congress Cataloging-in-Publication Data

Bryant-Mole, Karen.
    Does it bounce? / Karen Bryant-Mole.
      p. cm. — (Science buzzwords)
    Includes index.
    Summary: Illustrates words that describe actions and introduces words that relate to forces.
    ISBN 0-8368-1726-5 (lib. bdg.)
    1. Vocabulary—Juvenile literature. 2. Force and energy—Juvenile literature. [1. English language—Verb. 2. Vocabulary. 3. Force and energy.] I. Title. Series: Bryant-Mole, Karen. Science buzzwords.
PE1449.B79   1997
428.1—dc20   96-38739

First published in North America in 1997 by
Gareth Stevens Publishing
1555 North RiverCenter Drive, Suite 201
Milwaukee, WI 53212 USA

This edition © 1997 by Gareth Stevens, Inc. Original edition published in 1995 by A & C Black (Publishers) Limited, 35 Bedford Row, London, England, WC1R 4JH. Text © 1995 by Karen Bryant-Mole. Photographs © 1995 by Zul Mukhida, except pages 18, 19 Eye Ubiquitous. Additional end matter © 1997 by Gareth Stevens, Inc.

The author and publisher would like to thank all the children who appear in the photographs. They also wish to thank the Early Learning Centre, Swindon, for providing the equipment featured on pages 8, 9, 16, 17, and the title page.

Printed in the United States of America

1 2 3 4 5 6 7 8 9 01 00 99 98 97

SCIENCE BUZZWORDS

Does It Bounce?

Karen Bryant-Mole

Gareth Stevens Publishing
MILWAUKEE

go

Holly pedals her bike
to make it **go**.

stop

When she squeezes the brakes and puts
her feet on the ground, the bike **stops**.

float

Sam puts his boat in the water.
It **floats** on the top.

sink

Grace's car doesn't float.
It **sinks** to the bottom.

squeeze

When Yasmin **squeezes** the wet sponge,
water drips into the bucket.

spin

The clothes in Jess's washing machine
spin around and around.

lift

Grace has a toy telephone.
She **lifts** the receiver.

press

She **presses** the buttons and
pretends to call her friends.

heat

Holly's mom **heats** some
milk on the stove.

cool

It's too hot! Holly blows
on the milk to **cool** it.

twist

Sam **twists** the lid of
a jar to open it.

stir

Jess is making a cake. She **stirs**
the mixture with a big spoon.

backward

Holly drives her Jeep **backward**.
Drive carefully, Holly!

forward

It's much easier to drive **forward**.

roll

Nahid **rolls** the ball along the ground.
Will he knock down the pins?

bounce

Nahid loves to **bounce** up and
down on his trampoline.

fast

A race car moves quickly.
It is very **fast**.

slow

A snail takes a long time to move.
It is very **slow**.

push

Yasmin **pushes** the
wheelbarrow in front of her.

pull

Now she **pulls** the empty
wheelbarrow behind her.

throw

Jess **throws** a Frisbee.
It flies through the air.

catch

Grace **catches** the Frisbee
with both hands.

How to Use This Book

Children's understanding of concepts is fundamentally linked to their ability to comprehend and use relevant language. This book is designed to help children understand the vocabulary associated with **forces**.

Forces are important within the field of science. They provide one of the foundations upon which physics is built. Forces are responsible for the way an object moves or is moved.

Forces can be natural, like the push of water that enables an object to float; or they can be manufactured, like the power of a car's engine. The movement of our own bodies can produce forces, such as a *pull* on the handle of a wagon.

Understanding the ways in which forces can act on objects is an essential scientific skill. Forces can *push* or *pull* things, can make things *go* or *stop*, and can change the shape of things. This book helps children develop an understanding of this scientific concept by explaining key words connected with forces. It also encourages children to describe the actions they make.

Some of the pairs of words featured on each double page are opposites, such as *fast* and *slow*. Other pairs of words, such as *twist* and *stir*, however, are not opposites. Children can be encouraged to think about the words and to discuss which pairs are opposites and which are not.

Each word in this book is presented through a color photograph and a phrase, which uses the word in context. Besides explaining words that are basic to the understanding of forces, the book can be used in a number of other ways.

Children can think of a variety of situations, other than the ones shown in the photographs, that can be described using a particular Science Buzzword. For instance, the Buzzword *go* does not just describe the movement of a bike. It can be applied to several types of movement by many different objects. Cars, airplanes, boats, wheelchairs, trains, and horses all *go*.

Movements can be described more completely using multiple words. This book can help a child give a fuller description of movement. The movement of a toy wheelbarrow, for instance, might be described using the words *go*, *forward*, *push*, and *slow*.

Forces also influence the shape of objects. Children can use some of the Science Buzzwords in this book to consider the ways in which they use forces to change the shape of objects. For instance, clay can be *twisted* and *stretched*, cookie dough can be *rolled* and *cut*, and wet sand can be *pressed* and *molded*.

For Further Study —
Activities

1. **Model Making** — Make a model that can be *pushed* or *pulled*, that can go *backward* or *forward*, that can be *fast* or *slow*, and that can *go* or *stop*. You could make the base of your model from a shoebox.

2. **Play Dough** — See how many Science Buzzwords you can use when you play with Play Dough. Can you *roll* it, *twist* it, *press* it, and *squeeze* it? Think of some other words, such as *squash*, that describe ways of playing with Play Dough.

3. **Floaters and Sinkers** — Gather a collection of objects and see which objects *float* in water and which ones *sink*. A ball of modeling clay will *sink*. But can you find a way to change its shape to make it *float*?

4. **Frisbee "Golf"** — Make a simple Frisbee golf course in your backyard or a nearby park. Instead of nine holes, like on a golf course, use nine trees or other objects (like a swing set) that are close together for your targets. Count the number of times you have to throw the Frisbee to touch each of the nine targets.

5. **Ping-Pong Bounce** — Drop a Ping-Pong ball on a *hard* floor, like tile or wood, and see how high it bounces. Then put a piece of construction paper on the floor, and drop the ball from the same height. Does it bounce as high? Repeat this experiment on other surfaces, such as a pile of tissues or a dinner plate.

6. **Action Words** — Make a list of all of the Buzzwords in this book that describe an action, such as *float*, *squeeze*, and *lift*. Draw pictures to show the words, and see if a friend can guess what the words are. For example, you could draw the inside of a car for the word *drive*, a kangaroo for the word *hop*, or an airplane for the word *fly*.

7. **Charades** — This is a game you can play with your friends. Choose a Science Buzzword, and act it out without speaking. Your friends have to guess which Buzzword you have chosen.

8. **What's Cooking?** — Use Buzzwords as clues in a mystery recipe that you tell to a friend. For example, you could say, "First, *stir* flour and water in a bowl, and then *roll* it out flat. Put some tomato sauce and cheese on top, and *heat* it in the oven. What's cooking?"

9. **Stop and Go** — Play the game "Duck, Duck, Goose" using the Buzzwords *stop* and *go*. Have some friends sit in a circle facing each other. One person goes around the outside of the circle, saying *"stop"* (instead of "duck") as he or she taps the others. When the leader taps someone and says the Buzzword *"go,"* the person in the circle tries to "tag" the leader, who races around the circle to the empty spot.

Places to Visit

Betty Brinn Children's Museum
929 East Wisconsin Avenue
Milwaukee, WI 53202

Children's Museum
Museum Wharf
300 Congress Street
Boston, MA 02210

Children's Museum of Indianapolis
3000 North Meridian Street
Indianapolis, IN 46206

Discovery Place
301 North Tryon Street
Charlotte, NC 28202

Discovery World
712 West Wells Street
Milwaukee, WI 53233

Exploratorium
3601 Lyon Street
San Francisco, CA 94123

Los Angeles Children's Museum
310 North Main Street
Los Angeles, CA 90012

Museum of Science and Industry
57th Street and Lake Shore Drive
Chicago, IL 60637

Ontario Science Center
770 Don Mills Road
North York, Ontario M3C 1T3

Science Center of British Columbia
1455 Quebec Street
Vancouver, British Columbia V6A 3Z7

Science Museum Of Minnesota
30 East Tenth Street
St. Paul, MN 55101

The Smithsonian Institution
Information Center
1000 Jefferson Drive SW
Washington, D.C. 20560

Books

First Step Science (series). Kay Davies and Wendy Oldfield (Gareth Stevens)

Float and Sink. Maria Gordon (Thomas Learning)

Hands-On Science (series). (Gareth Stevens)

The Kids Science Book. Robert Hirshfield and Nancy White (Williamson)

Magic Mud and Other Great Experiments. Gordon Penrose (Little Simon)

The Magic School Bus: Science Explorations. (Scholastic)

Make It Change. David Evans (Dorling Kindersley)

My First Science Book. Angela Wilkes (Knopf)

Pushing and Pulling. Gary Gibson (Copper Beech Books)

Silly Science. Shar Levine and Leslie Johnstone (John Wiley & Sons)

Simple Science Projects (series). John Williams (Gareth Stevens)

Web Sites

http://www.waterw.com/~science/kids.html

http://www.islandnet.com/~yesmag/

Videos

Floating and Sinking. (Journal Films and Video)

Movement Everywhere. (Encyclopædia Britannica Educational Corporation)

Moving A Hippo. (Children's Television International)

Push and Pull: Simple Machines At Work. (Rainbow Educational Video)

What Makes Things Move?
    (Encyclopædia Britannica Educational Corporation)

Index